M

is for

Money Magick

Kitchen Table Magick Series

by

G. Alan Joel

ISBN-13: 979-8985625776

Email: ***alan@shamanschool.com***
Website: ***www.shamanschool.com***

Publisher: Esoteric School of Shamanism and Magic, Inc.

Disclaimer and Legal Notice:
The Esoteric School of Shamanism and Magic has made every effort to ensure, at the time of this writing, that the information contained in this book is as accurate as possible. The publisher and author make no warranties or representation with respect to the completeness, fitness, accuracy, applicability, or appropriateness of this book's contents. This book's information is provided strictly for entertainment and educational purposes. Should you choose to use or apply the ideas provided in this book, you take full responsibility for your own actions. The publisher and author provide no guarantee that your life will improve in any way should you choose to use the information presented in this book. The ability of the information provided in this book to provide self-help and life improvement to the reader is entirely dependent upon the reader. The reader's ability to gain positive results from the information presented in this book is entirely dependent on the amount of time the reader devotes to the application of the material in this book, the willingness of the reader to dedicate time and effort to learning the materials presented in this book, as well as the reader's own belief system, which may help or hinder the reader's ability to benefit from this book's materials. Since each reader differs according to willingness and openness to the information available in this book, the author and publisher cannot guarantee success or improvement for every individual reader. Neither the publisher nor the author assumes responsibility for the reader's actions, or whether the information is used for negative or positive purposes. The information contained in this book is drawn from tribal traditions—both modern and ancient—as well as the author's 30 plus years' experience researching and teaching this material to students. The information in this book is presented as interpreted by the author, and, as such, may or may not be entirely accurate. In no way should the information presented in this book be a substitute for advice from health or mental health professionals. The author and publisher are not liable—or in any way responsible—for actions

[this page intentionally left blank]

Money Magick Blessing

Child of Wonder,
Child of Flame,
Nourish My Spirit, and
Protect My Aim.

If you need money now,
Listen close as I tell you how.
With money magick by your side,
Manifestation occurs by and by.

'Tis the right of all beings who on this planet live,
To have access to prosperity, to have and to give.
The magickal alignment of emotion and thought,
Be a most powerful tool for the prosperity sought.

Clarity is most important according to magickal lore,
Plus, the help of Angels, Guides, Totems, and more!
Give to get makes the wealth go round,
As does a self-chosen price for your prosperity to abound!

Mantras and meditation quiet to monkey mind,
So that Spirit steps forth with wealth to unbind.
All needed magick we have within,
As magickal beings we be, though thick and through thin!

Thus, my will, so mote it be!

[this page intentionally left blank]

Free Gift

To thank you for purchasing this book, I'd like to give you a

100% FREE GIFT

Learn more about your free magickal gift.

Access Your Free Gift at
www.shamanschool.com

Find a complete list of magickal resources on https://amzn.to/3swxvPo. These resources are constantly updated so check back often!

Kitchen Table Money Magick
Table of Contents

[this page intentionally left blank]

Introduction to Kitchen Table Money Magick

"We're asking you to trust in the Well-being. In optimism there is magic."
~ Abraham

A Note About This Introduction

This book is one of a series of books in the Kitchen Table Magick series. Each book in the series addresses a specific area of magick (love, money, psychic development, etc.), and is written in a simple "recipe" format for people who want to use magick in their lives immediately. The Kitchen Table Magick series is akin to a Julia Childs recipe book, only these books contain magickal recipes for people to cook up some miraculous and magickal manifestations in their lives.

Because this series was designed so that each person could pick and choose to read just the books that pertain to their current life situation, each book is meant to be readable as a stand-alone book. To introduce the new reader to the series, this introduction to the series is repeated at the beginning of each book. If you have already read one or more books in this series, please feel free to jump ahead to the recipes that interest you. At the same time, some people feel that reviewing the introduction, as well as the "Rules and Tips," is helpful before diving in. In magickal circles, your will is the guideline so choose whichever route best suits you... the Universe and magickal beings will follow!

What is Magick?

Many people have multiple different ideas about what magick is or can be. For the sake of clarity, here is what we know about magick after more than 35 years of study and practice. Magick is a precision science! It is also:

- The science of deliberate creation.
- The science of effective prayer.
- The science of manifesting Higher Will (substitute whatever Higher Force is most familiar to you) on the energetic and material planes.
- The science of heightened awareness, selective perception, and dynamic, harmonious relationships.
- The study of intention (as per Aleister Crowley, one of the greatest magickal practitioners in history).
- The system of creation, not coercion. Note: The word manipulation is often used in conjunction with magick, but manipulation simply means the use of the hands. It should be an "OK" word without a lot of charge, but currently it is used mostly to mean coercion. Look it up!
- The principle that every intentional act is a magickal act! Magick gives us the ability to communicate with beings on all levels, and allows us to understand, through direct experience, the actual workings of the Universe.
- The traditional path of spiritual growth.
- Not extraordinary knowledge. It is the "normal" way of life. We've just lost access to it. When you have this kind of knowledge in your understanding, you have the ability to resolve spiritual questions that otherwise become catechism. From a magickal point of view, catechism is not acceptable, since a practitioner must

experience and verify everything for him or herself. It avoids the trap of dogma. In past times, having a magickal foundation was essential so that we could talk directly to higher beings in the Universal hierarchy.

- Necessary to effective religious practice.

There is some confusion as to how to spell the word "magick." There are three different commonly used spellings: magick, magic, and majick. Eliphas Levi first used the form "magick" to differentiate religious or ceremonial from stage magick. All forms of spelling are acceptable in what this author teaches.

"I love Kitchen Table Magick! It's the best mix of both mystical and down-to-earth magick I have ever encountered. The fact that I can use items from my pantry is so handy and fun! It literally is about cooking up magick at my kitchen table, and having love show up in the least expected places!"

~ Wendy J., Skokie, IL

Is Magick Real?

Yes. Magick is very real and has existed as a precise science for thousands of years. Whether you use the word magick or another name, this spiritual practice is very real. Every single person can learn to do magick. We are ALL born with the talents and abilities that empower us to do magick. The only reason that magick seems so, well, magickal is that this society no longer teaches the art and science of magick. In the distant past, magickal study was just as important as math, science, or the arts. In fact, magick was and still is the birthright of EVERY planetary citizen.

Can you learn to do the kind of magick portrayed in the movies? Yes... and no. The movies are great at giving you a taste of what you can do with magick, but they are not very accurate. In the Harry Potter movies, for instance, the characters use their Wands for every magickal operation. In reality, you can only use the Wand to handle Air energies. Your Wand would actually explode or catch fire if you tried to use it to throw Firebolts and Fireballs as the characters do in the movie.

So, what can you actually do with magick? Quite a lot. Here is a short list to get you started:

- Balance your energies for healing and manifestation
- Change old beliefs
- Defend yourself against physical and psychic attack
- Heal yourself and others
- Find hidden information and see possible futures (and change the future if you do not like the probable futures you divine)
- Psychically communicate with other beings
- Create sacred space
- Find lost people and objects
- Manifest what you want and need in life

At the very basis of magick is the understanding of the four elements: Air, Fire, Water, and Earth. Called elemental magick, these foundational elements are real. Air, Fire, Water, and Earth are part of our natural everyday environment. What makes them magickal is the understanding of how they operate not just on the physical level, but also at the levels of Mind and Spirit.

For instance, while on the physical level, Air is just the stuff we breathe. On the magickal levels Air is the conduit of psychic communication, enlightenment, understanding, dreaming, and more. If you want more of these things in your life, then you need more magickal Air. How do you get more magickal Air? Wear more Air colors, including white for communication and sky blue for enlightenment and understanding. To take this one step further, you could also use various magickal techniques to take on more Air to make your body lighter. Take on enough Air and you'll be able to levitate.

By just extending your understanding and use of the basic ingredients of nature, you are doing magick! Seen in this light, magick isn't all smoke and mirrors, nor is it the result of Hollywood special effects. Magick is the result of truly understanding and working with the very elements that are all around you.

One final note: Many masters, including Wayne Dyer, have said, "You'll see it when you believe it." The same is true for magick. In other words, the suspension of disbelief and the willingness not to exercise contempt prior to investigation are requirements for magick to be "real." Magick is all around us, and always is, but our ability to perceive and use the forces of magick depends on our willingness to be open. No one else can show it to you, only your direct experience and observation can "prove" or demonstrate to you that magick is real.

[this page intentionally left blank]

What is Kitchen Table Magick?

Kitchen Table Magick is exactly what it sounds like—a series of simple recipes that you can literally "cook up" at your kitchen table using household ingredients from your own pantry and cupboard.

The Kitchen Table Magick books have been created for ordinary people who want to mix up a little magick in their lives without all the fancy rituals, but simply with everyday ingredients that can be found in the kitchen pantry, bathroom medicine cabinet, or even stuffed in the back of the junk drawer.

The goal of these books is to allow anyone with the desire to learn this craft to mix up magick literally at the kitchen table using simple recipes. What goes into a simple recipe?

- Everyday items as ingredients
- Easy to follow instructions that don't require years of training
- Procedures that take less than two hours from start to finish
- Built-in expertise that allows the magick to do the heavy lifting
- Some friendly advice on how you can help your magickal recipe provide the best results
- Oh, and a few little rules and guidelines about magickal practice in this specific arena that will keep you safe and sound, magickally speaking, when you use these recipes

Kitchen Table Magick Equals:
Quick – Effective – Safe – Everyday Use – Ordinary Affordable Ingredients

Why Use Kitchen Table Magick?

- Everyone can do magick.
- Magick should be simple, effective, and start working right away, else it is not magick.
- Not everyone has the time or resources to enroll in a school.
- People ask us for magickal help in hundreds of emails everyday... Kitchen Table Magick is designed to help these very people.
- Of the many areas of life, most people only seem to need help in one or two areas, so you need only buy those Kitchen Table Magick books that apply to your needs.
- Magick is for the masses, and should be accessible, affordable, and simple to do. This is what our teacher taught us, and this is the legacy we are paying forward as well.
- While there are many more advanced forms of magick, these books are an introduction to that world so that you can dabble, experiment, try things out, see the result, adjust and amend, and generally have fun... just as you would cooking a meal in your kitchen.
- This book is not for the major foodie, but it is perfect for the person who needs magickal help right here, right now!

Who Should Use These Recipes?

- You and anyone you know who would like a little more magick and a little less ordinary reality in their lives.
- Anyone who needs help RIGHT now and doesn't have time to fly to India or Sedona to sit at the feet of a guru.

- Anyone who does not have access to anything but a computer for help and guidance.
- Anyone who wants to do magick and then forget it (all while quietly watching the magick "do its thing").
- Anyone who wants affordable, down to earth magick they can do with regular ingredients in the comfort of home.

When to Use Kitchen Table Magick: Anytime...

- You need help.
- You don't want to do all the heavy lifting (leave that to the Angels, Spirit Guides, Animal Totems, and so forth).
- You seem stuck in a rut or corner with no way out.
- You've been struggling with a problem for a long time and need a resolution.
- You don't know what to do but you need to do SOMETHING.
- You'd like to learn how to practice the craft.
- You want to live a more magickal life and stop dealing with ordinary hassles all the time.

How Do We Know These Recipes Work?

- We teach a slew of these recipes in one-day workshops all over the country, via teleconference, and via videoconference. We also email them to people as part of our school's service work, or post them on our blogs and articles library.
- We have used them for over 35 years and still do, every single day – literally tested out at our own kitchen tables for over 35 years (and at thousands of kitchen tables around the world) for a quarter century or more.
- We receive all kinds of stories and testimonials from happy successful students.

[this page intentionally left blank]

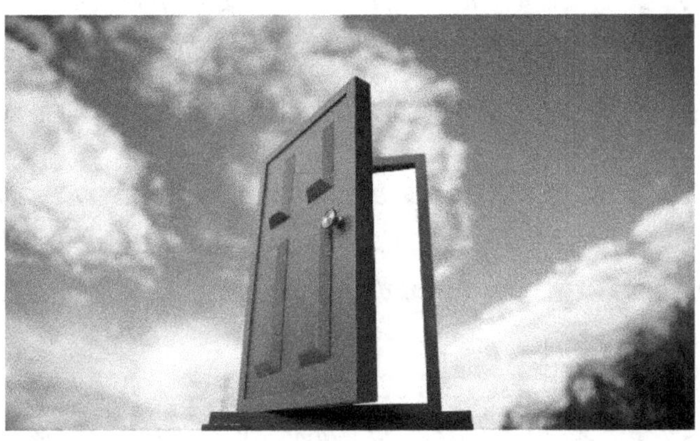

Kitchen Table Money Magick at Work…

Read the following example to discover how Money Magick works in real life…

Money Magick Has Many Faces

Before I started taking online classes from the Esoteric School of Shamanism and Magic, I had tried my hand at several "money spells." Those spells never resulted in any money, so I stopped believing in the power of magick to attract money into my life.

With those money spells, I always asked for a lump sum of cash, which never manifested. I didn't know what I was doing wrong until I learned how to properly do magickal rituals and spells. I discovered that my previous spells lacked several key factors, including:

- *Clarity about the specific details (such as safeguards, purpose, and time frame)*

- *Enough "wiggle room" to allow the Universe to manifest my request in the easiest possible way*
- *A detailed examination of any beliefs that would impede the spell*
- *The understanding that money doesn't always have to be a lump sum of cash (many other options are available)*

During the Esoteric School's Basic Magick class, I could hardly wait for the spellwork portion. I wanted to discover what I was doing to wrong, and why my money spells never manifested any money. Finally, we began to work on our spells. As usual, I wrote up a money spell. Before I launched it, we had a class discussion about our past experiences with spells. I shared that no money spell had ever worked for me. My teacher helped me correct my spell (to offset the key factors I mentioned previously) so it had the greatest chance for success. After, I was both grateful and excited to launch my spell.

Imagine my surprise when my teacher suggested that I not launch my spell! What? My teacher suggested that I had built up a resistant belief about money and magick. After so many failed spells, my thoughts and emotions around this kind of spellwork would prevent the Universe from delivering the money I sought.

To work around my resistance, my teacher suggested that I create a different kind of money spell. Instead of asking for a lump sum of money, perhaps I could write a spell to change my lifestyle so that my expenses were significantly reduced. My teacher guided me to leave the "how" portion of the spell open to the Universe (so long as safeguards were written to prevent unpleasant surprises).

So, I wrote up my spell following my teacher's guidance. I was prepared to wait a long time (or forever) because money spells had never worked for me before. But I admit that I was also curious about this "new" approach to money spells.

Less than three weeks after I launched my spell, I received a call from my aunt, who lived in the same town as me. She was aging and needed help with activities of daily living, such as driving, bathing, cleaning, cooking, shopping, and so on. She asked me to move in with her, and she also offered to pay me—and pay me well with tax-free dollars. My aunt was enrolled in both state and federal programs that paid for a live-in caregiver.

Wow! My aunt and I get along "like a house on fire" (as the saying goes), so I took her up on her offer immediately. I was able to go to work during the day and take care of my aunt before I left for work, during lunch, and at night. Immediately the expenses for my room and board disappeared because I moved in with my aunt. I was able to return my leased car because I could use my aunt's car, both to get to work and to drive my aunt around. No car payment, no car insurance.

To top it all off, my aunt was so grateful that she offered to pay for a membership at a rock-climbing gym—rock climbing was my hobby and chosen form

of stress relief! Long story short? My money magick spell worked like a charm, thanks to a proper education in how to write a spell. Now I love to write spells in unique ways so that I can see how the Universe will manifest them in my life. In fact, the process of creating magick in my life is just as much fun as seeing the results! I love money magick… and all magick done well and done right!
~ Barbara G., Milton, GA

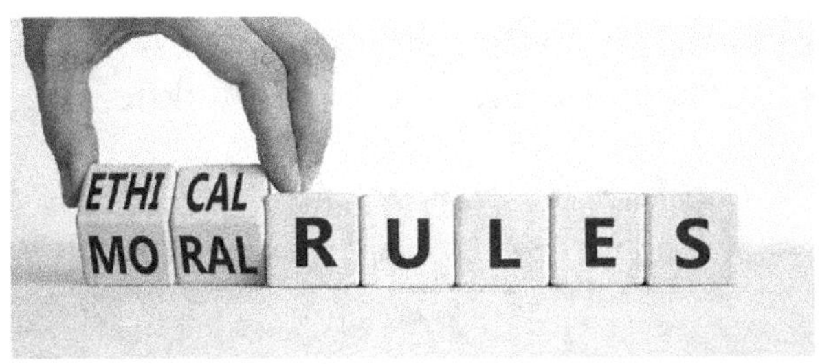

A Few Rules and Tips About Kitchen Table Magick

As with any game, the game of life has its own set of rules. Specifically, the spiritual side of life has rules. Play by those rules and you will stay safe and easily attract what you want into your life. Break those rules and all types of unwanted consequences happen.

These "spiritual rules" are ones that have been observed, both in personal spiritual practice and spiritual practice with various associated groups and teachers. These rules universally govern any spiritual practice and appear to be in effect whether you know them or not. Unlike ethics and morals, which change with culture and time, these spiritual rules appear to have remained the same throughout time, unchanging, like physical and scientific rules.

The rules in the following section are adapted from *Rules of the Road*, as created by George Dew, co-founder of the Church of Seven Arrows. There are two major rules, which are common to most spiritual practices, along with some minor rules that are specific to our form of magickal practice.

Two Major Rules

These two rules will probably sound familiar, as they appear in most major religions and spiritual practices, most probably because they are common-sense and apply not just to spiritual practice, but to life as well.

First Rule: Golden Rule or Law of Karma

This first rule is literally a "golden oldie":

> *What you do to the environment or to other beings in the environment brings similar effects back to you in your life.*

Often recognized as the Golden Rule or the Law of Karma, this rule tops the list because it reminds all spiritual practitioners of potential unwanted "rebound" or side effects. As your spiritual power, focus, and abilities grow, this rule will have an ever-greater impact on your life unless you exercise caution. The Universe responds more strongly and powerfully to those with focus, power, and ability.

Note: As humanity moves further in the Aquarian Age, many spiritual practitioners have seen more effects from this rule occur faster. In the past, effects of this rule that often took lifetimes to manifest now occur in minutes, days, weeks, or months. In this particular time in Earth's history, karma seems to operate under a "pay as you go" system. Simply stated, expect the effects of the Law of Karma to occur quickly.

Second Rule: The Judgment of "Good and Bad" According to the Universe

This second rule adds clarity and detail to the first rule described previously:

> *If you are unsure whether your acts are "good or bad"--that is, whether those acts are in keeping with universal laws on this planet—the Universe will reflect its judgment back to you quickly, according to the "pay as you go" Law of Karma.*

This law holds as true for individuals as it does for entire communities, states, nations, or other organized groups. If you are still unsure of the feedback you receive from the Universe, check areas such as your level of health, the soundness of social relationships, your prosperity or lack of, sufficiency of various needs in life, and even your "luck" with appliances and machines. If your luck appears to be consistently poor, then you are probably acting contrary to universal governing laws, regardless of your intentions. The Universe cares about what you do more than what you intend.

Additional Detailed Rules

The following rules offer more detailed standards by which to measure your acts or the acts of others to determine whether these acts are in accordance with universal laws.

- Do nothing that will harm another being unless you are willing to suffer similar or greater harm. What the Universe considers "harm" may be different than what you consider harm.
- Do not bind another being unless you are willing to be similarly bound. An example of binding someone is doing acts in attempt to coerce a specific other person to love you. There is no problem with attracting your soul mate into your life, but doing acts that attempt to coerce a specific other person to love you is a type of binding.
- Never use your spiritual abilities in vain, to show off, or to boost your pride. Using your spiritual abilities from a place of pride usually causes the Universe to bring instant backlash into your life.
- If you choose to charge money or barter for using your spiritual abilities in the service of others, avoid charging extremely high prices. Charge prices for using methods comparable to other professionals, such as an attorney or accountant.
- Never use any spiritual word, chant, litany, or similar "device" unless you are confident in your understanding of its methods, intents, and effects.
- When undertaking a major spiritual operation—one that will require significant effort or attempts to

create a major effect in the world—use divination to determine whether you can safely benefit from such an operation, and to discover the obstacles you must overcome. Divination methods such as pendulum readings, channeling, meditation, and question circles (to name a few) can reveal hidden factors of which you may be unaware.

- In any spiritual endeavor, take your time, think it through, and do it right!

The good news is that you can still use money magick rituals. The ones we teach in this book won't get you in trouble with the Universe, yet will still allow you to use money magick to manifest money in your life. The rituals in this book will also help you create space so the Universe can work freely and easily to bring your desired results to you!

The Ingredients of Money Magick

"Money won't create success, the freedom to make it will."
~ Nelson Mandela

More money. Easier access to money. Simpler ways to attract money. Rarely has there been a person who has not wished money would come more easily into their life. This book is all about granting that wish. The rituals in this book provide simple yet effective magical rituals to transform your relationship with money so it comes into your life in better ways—with more ease and speed, and in greater quantity.

Just as relationships between people can go sour, so can relationships with other items or concepts, such as health, career, and money. To change your relationship to anything simply requires you tell yourself a different story about it.

Since the Universe responds to your intention and vibration, what you believe "is". No matter how much is in your bank account, if you feel wealthy and believe you are and always will be wealthy, your bank account will reflect that feeling and belief. On the other hand, if you are always short of money, then you need to look at the "story" you tell yourself about money. It is also useful to examine how your vibration about money attracts the amount and longevity of money in your life.

The recipes in this book present exercises and rituals for you to perform that will:

- Change your relationship with money
- Change the story you tell yourself about your abundance or lack of money
- Teach you how to work with Higher Powers and Beings to open the way for the Universe to deliver more money to you

Money Magick Appetizer Recipes

Appetizers: Learning "How and Why" with Magick and Money

Create a New Relationship with Money with a Magickal Universe Box

Getting Answers with Gaining Financial Freedom from a Question Circle

"The whys and wherefores of money have always been a mystery for me. Sometimes it seems like I can manifest money easily in my life.... Other times money has been out of reach. With the Question Circle and Magickal Box, I was able to clarify what I really wanted, AND communicate it to the Universe! Now the Universe always seems to hear me now. How awesome is that?"
~ Sally U., Ogden,, UT

[this page intentionally left blank]

Create a New Relationship with Money with a Magickal Universe Box

"Your conclusion that there isn't enough of something—whether it is enough land, or money, or clarity—stems from you learning, without meaning to, a vibration that holds you apart from what you want. There is no limitation. If you identify a desire for it, Source recognizes your desire, and immediately begins to deliver it to you. And it will manifest in the variety, in the fullness, and in the way that you, and only you, learn to allow it."
~ Abraham

Time Required: Sixty Minutes

To bring more money into your reality, start changing the way you think about money. Move your focus to what money can do for you rather than how to get money for its own sake. For instance, if you want to take a trip to a foreign country but sit around feeling depressed that you don't have the money to do so, you will never gain the money to fund that trip. Instead, shift your focus to the trip itself, which is the end goal of having the money. Focus on where you will go, what you will see, what attractions you will visit and so on. Then start preparing for the trip and envision yourself on the trip. In doing so, you will be more likely to live in an excited, fizzy, and happy state of being. This mood will help you attract the money that you need.

Ingredients

- A goal for which you need to attract money to accomplish.
- A box (or small chest) and fun items with which to decorate it (i.e., pictures from magazines, markers, paint, other pictures, colored paper, and more)
- Paper and pen or pencil

Recipe Directions

1. Adopt the slogan "Act as if you already have what you want."

2. Make a list for the Universe of exactly what you want. If you want to go on a trip, then write a list that might include where you want to go, the dates you want to go on the trip, and other details (such as length of trip, how much spendable money you want to have, first class airfare, etc.).

3. Create a "Universe Box," by applying pictures, colored paper, paint, markers, and other items that represent your goal. Decorate your box until it becomes something fun, fancy, and whimsical into which you will put your wishes that you want the Universe to fulfill. Once you have made your box, attach the following magical verse to it:

"Ask and ye shall receive,
Needing only to trust and believe

For the abundance that I seek,
With the Universe I now speak.
Into this magical box I place,
Requests for desires to enter my space.
Replace the unwanted with the list I have made,
Trusting that the Universe will come to my aid."

4. Hold the box between your hands, and magickally "key" it by running energy from your dominant hand (the one with which you point) to your other hand. Then move the energy up the arm of your non-dominant hand, across your shoulders, and back to your dominant hand again. Say the magickal verse in a voice of command three times as you continue flowing energy between your hands. Once you are done, you have a magickal box with which to communicate with the Universe.

5. Put your list in the box and put the box in the safest and most sacred place you can find. This might be an altar or designated sacred space, such as a meditation room.

6. Now you have "placed your order" and are ready to act as if you already have what you want. Put that slogan into action and get busy preparing for your trip. You might start packing your suitcase, checking baggage requirements with the airlines, get forms from the Post Office to be ready to submit for a "mail hold" while you are gone, start the process of getting a passport if you don't have one and will need one for your destination, and so forth.

7. Keep yourself busy and out of the way while the Universe works on your manifestation. You will feel a deep sense of satisfaction which creates energy that will help the Universe deliver your request even faster. Whenever doubt creeps in, hold your magickally-

keyed Universe box and repeat the magickal verse while flowing energy between your hands (in the same way as you have previously). This reinforces your request to the Universe and relieves your doubt.

8. Stick with your preparations for the trip in the belief that it is happening, but avoid doing direct actions that could be interpreted as “working toward” the trip. For example, do not go get a second job to help pay for the trip, sell your personal items to get extra money, or borrow money from friends or family. Delivering the money for the trip is the Universe’s job and it only needs you to allow it to bring it to you magickally.

How to Use the Results of Your Recipe

Remember that real magick doesn’t happen overnight; you must give the Universe time to work. This concept can be difficult for many people, and they become impatient waiting for the Universe to deliver. This impatience gets in the way of the flow of money from coming to you. Anytime you become frustrated with waiting and are tempted to take action to make your manifestation happen, STOP! Ask yourself, “Do I want this to happen by magick or by blood, sweat, and tears?” The choice is yours. Return to your Universe box anytime you feel doubt, fear, or frustration. If you want to allow magick to work in your life, then take specific actions that you will have to take anyway when your dream manifests. Do NOT take actions that you would normally take if magick didn't exist. In other words, it would be much better to spend your energy “packing your bags!”

Getting Answers with Gaining Financial Freedom from a Question Circle

"It's good to have money and the things that money can buy, but it's good, too, to check up once in a while and make sure that you haven't lost the things that money can't buy."
~ George Horace Lorimer

Time Required: Sixty Minutes

The good news about creating a new relationship with money is that you don't have to do it alone. You can literally call upon any and all spiritual guides you like. If you work with a specific patron saint or angel or Universal helper, then you can ask for their help to show you roadblocks, stumbling points, or help you discover why you are not attracting money or those things you desire money to bring you. Whether you already have a magical helper or not, you can use this recipe to get guidance and help from the four cardinal directions (East, South, West, and North) by using a Question Circle. A question circle is an easy way to contact and communicate with the beings of the four directions to get multiple perspectives on a problem or issue in your life.

Ingredients

- A clean dark blue or brown glass dropper bottle (one ounce size)
- Pure spring water
- A small amount of alcohol to stabilize the flower essence mixtures (brandy or vodka work well, and you only need a few drops)
- A pen, a small piece of paper, and tape to label your bottle
- The willingness and patience to play around with different essences until you find some that work for you

Recipe Directions

1. You can employ many different methods when choosing your flower essences. One way is to scan the following list and choose one or more that seem most likely to help you experience and remember useful dreams (dreams that contain information you want or need). Another method is to list all of the following flower essences on a sheet a paper and number them in sequence, starting at 1. Then write the numbers on small slips of paper, placing the slips face down on a table. Take a few moments to center yourself with some deep breathing or meditation. Then, look at the slips of paper and choose the ones that attract you. Some will appear brighter, or some may have an active energetic pull. Select one or more numbers until you feel complete. Finally, turn over the numbers and consult the numbered list of flower essences. The corresponding essences are the ones that will go into your flower essence mixture.

- ***Angelica***: This flower essence puts you in touch with Spirit helpers, especially when you feel the need for spiritual guidance or protection. This essence is wonderful if you feel shut down or out of touch with the spiritual world.
- ***Dill***: If have difficulty getting into a dream state, or you are a restless sleeper, then this flower essence can help you greatly. Dill calms the senses, and helps you shed the frenetic energy of the day. This flower essence creates a sacred space while you are sleeping so that you can hear your Spirit guides through your dreams.
- ***Lotus***: The reason that the Lotus flower is so prominent in many religions (especially Eastern religions) is because this flower opens the seventh chakra. This chakra, once opened, allows spiritual energy to enter the physical and energetic body. The awakening of the seventh chakra is often associated with enlightenment in many cultures. For those who wish for enlightened information through dreams, Lotus is a perfect solution.
- ***Potato:*** Sometimes it can be difficult to be both dreamer and pragmatist. Or, more specifically, it can be difficult to translate the information you receive in your dreams into practical action steps that will help you achieve your goals. Potato is an excellent flower essence to help you keep one foot in each world—the dream world and the waking everyday world. Potato is one of the best flower essences for "bridging" the two worlds.
- ***Rock Rose***: This flower essence is a one of the ingredients in Rescue Remedy. Specifically, this essence is useful for clearing nightmares, night terrors, and past traumatic events. Rock Rose also helps whenever you are frozen by fear, perfectionism, or trauma.
- ***Star Tulip***: This flower essence is sometimes called Cat's Ear and can be useful if you typically

dream of mundane events (running errands, daily tasks, and events from recent days). Star Tulip helps you become more sensitive to messages from Spirit and other helpers, raising the level of dream vibrations so you that you receive enlightened and useful higher-level guidance.

- ***Wormwood***: If you know that you dream but have a difficult time remembering enough dream fragments to record in your dream diary, Wormwood can help. This flower essence can help you extend the state of twilight consciousness so you gather and record more dream fragments.

2. If you don't feel like mixing your own flower essences, you can also choose pre-mixed remedies, such as Rescue Remedy or specific commercial remedies for dream enhancement.

3. Once you have your chosen flower essences (they are most commonly stored in one-ounce bottles), gather the other necessary ingredients: your own glass bottle, spring water, and the alcohol of your choice (many people prefer flavored brandies).

4. Open your dropper bottle and fill it ¾ full with spring water. Add four to eight drops of each flower essence you wish to add to your mix. Top off the mixture with seven to eleven drops of alcohol. Screw the dropper top back on the bottle.

5. Holding the bottle in your dominant hand, pound the bottom of the bottle on the palm of your other hand at least 50 times. This is called succussing the flower essence. This step not only mixes the ingredients in the bottle but increases the potency of the flower essences.

6. Using your pen, paper, and tape, label your bottle with the ingredients of your mixture, the purpose of the mixture, the date, and your name. Note the date you start using your flower essence in your dream diary. This will help you assess the effectiveness of your flower remedy.

7. Now your flower essence is ready to use. You can take four to eight drops at night just before bed, you can add four to eight drops in your water bottle (and sip on the bottle throughout the day), or you can just take four to eight drops of the flower essence by itself throughout the day.

8. If you use your flower essence frequently, you don't have to start from scratch if you want to continue using the mixture. Simply top up your bottle to ¾ full with spring water, and add seven to 11 drops of brandy or other alcohol. Succuss the mixture at least 50 times. At this point you once more have a full bottle. Because flower essences of vibrational essences, those vibrations stay in the mixture. By adding water and alcohol, and succussing the mixture, you spread the vibration throughout the bottle with no loss in the effect or force of your flower essence mixture.

How to Use the Results of Your Recipe

In your dream diary record any changes, no matter how small, that you experience in your dream life. This will show you whether your flower essence is a good match for what you seek in your dreams. If the mixture doesn't seem to work, you can create a new essence and see if that helps enhance your dreams. You can also take your dream flower remedy more frequently. You can also research flower remedies for dreams on your own, online or in books. Finally, you can opt to purchase a pre-mixed flower remedy that has good reviews for the type of "dream help" that you seek. Sometimes a flower essence that is effective for many people will be more effective because of the 100th monkey principle (meaning that the more people that use the remedy, the more strongly those vibrations will exist on the planet. By taking that same remedy, you are, in essence, tapping into that powerful river of vibrations. This can add the power needed for breakthroughs and enlightenment from dreams!

Money Magick Main Course Recipes

Main Courses: Paying it Forward

Get Clear About What You Want and Attract It: Magickal Directions to the Universe

Pay Some Energy Forward to Be Returned Tenfold: Magickal Come Along

Pay Some Energy Forward to Be Returned Tenfold: Pick a Price to Pay

"Money won't create success, the freedom to make it will."

~ Nelson Mandela

[this page intentionally left blank]

Get Clear About What You Want and Attract It: Magickal Directions to the Universe

"A little thought and a little kindness are often worth more than a great deal of money."
~ John Ruskin

Time Required: Sixty Minutes

Since the Universe will deliver what you ask for by taking the path of least resistance, you need to be specific about what you want and what you don't to happen in manifesting your desire – i.e. – money. This recipe will help you develop a list that in practice we call Directors and Limiters. The recipe following this one will give you two energetic ways to send these requirements out to the Universe.

Ingredients

- Paper and pen or pencil.
- Your "thinking cap".

Recipe Directions

1. Pick a time to be able to sit quietly without distractions.

2. Focus on what it is you want to manifest, for example a certain amount of money.

3. Start writing down a list that specifies the things you want to achieve and areas or conditions you want to avoid.

4. Your list should include the purpose, safeguards, and when to start and stop or what the period of time you need the manifestation to occur is. For example, to get a new job you might write the job description, amount of pay, type of company you want to be involved with, what kinds of benefits are involved, when you want the new job to start, the type of boss you want, what city the job must be in, and so forth.

5. Specify in your list what you want and do not want but do not tell how it is to be done or be so limiting as to not allow the Universe the room to work. The how is the magick that will come from the Universe.

6. If you specify some type of number in your directors and limiters, do so with a range instead of an exact number to allow the Universe more freedom to achieve the goal and make sure you ask for goals that are reasonable. Asking for $10,000 immediately is not a reasonable goal as there is no time included for the Universe to gather force to get to a solution. Real magick doesn't work that way.

7. In the case of attracting money here is a sample of magickal directions that you might write:

    - Bring me at least $10,000.00 in 4 to 5 weeks, by (date), (year), and not more than one million dollars by (date), (year).
    - No harm shall come to anyone, nor untimely death, nor loss of property as a result of this manifestation.
    - Whatever money shall come as a result of this manifestation shall be free and clear, with no strings attached and not obtained by illegal means.
    - The money will be used to pay off debts, to start my new career, and to purchase a house.
    - The achievement of this goal is open to support, help, and empowerment from angels and higher beings that can make a positive contribution.
    - My attitudes and fears will not have an adverse effect on the accomplishment of this manifestation.

How to Use the Results of Your Recipe

By putting much thought into your Directors and Limiters you will be giving the Universe a clear picture of what you want to happen and what you do not want to happen. Take a lesson from the student who manifested the money she wanted but at the cost of her husband dying in order for her to collect the life insurance. This was not what she intended, but she did not write this into her Limiters so the Universe saw this scenario as the quickest and easiest way to deliver the money she asked for. Write your magickal list of directions and then look at the next recipe for a way to use them to attract what you want.

[this page intentionally left blank]

Pay Some Energy Forward to Be Returned Tenfold: Magickal Come Along

"He is rich or poor according to what he is, not according to what he has."
~Henry Ward Beecher

Time Required: Sixty Minutes

Come Alongs are a type of magickal spell using your Plate (the Earth tool) and a magnet or candle to bring things to you. You can do this operation with a Sun Candle or with a magnet and this recipe will give you both variations.

Ingredients (one or all of the items below)

- The list of Directors and Limiters you made in the last recipe.
- A keyed Plate (magickal Earth element tool).
- A Sun Yellow candle and wooden or paper matches

OR a large magnet.

- Before you begin this recipe, you need to select a Plate (magickal Earth element tool) and key it. To key it you will also need the magickal tools Firebowl and Chalice (Water element tool) and be able to "charge" them.

Choosing a Plate (Magickal Earth element tool)
Your Plate should:

- Be made of wood, ceramic or porcelain. Glass or metal will also work.
- Be colored with Earth tones or have plant-based designs in Earth tones. Be sure that the patterns are not carved very deeply into the plate.
- Be six to ten inches in diameter which is slightly larger than a salad plate. You should be able to hold it easily by placing your thumbs in the center of the plate and the rest of your fingers on the edge.
- Be round in shape for even energy flow and slightly dished in the center.

Firebowl: When choosing a Firebowl, look for one that is made of brass, cast-iron, ceramic or a hard hardwood. It should be 4-6 inches in diameter and 4-5 inches deep. It should also be a shape that is easily held with one or both hands and light enough to carry in one hand if necessary. Make sure your Firebowl is of a shape that will be stable when placed on a flat surface. The shape of the bowl should also be curved-in and flared back out at the top rim to promote "columning" of incense or smoke. Fill it with ground fire clay or clean, fine sand. Non-scented cat litter (which is ground clay) works well as long as it does not have chemicals or deodorants in it. Put 1-2 inches in the bottom of your Firebowl as an insulator to protect the Firebowl itself, your hands and any surfaces from the heat.

To charge the Firebowl you will need:

- Self-starting charcoal disks.

- Wooden or paper matches.
- Pine resin.
- Sage.
- Fine wood shavings.
- Sun Yellow candle.

Charging the Firebowl to program it for keying your plate:

- Light your Sun Yellow candle with a wooden or paper match.
- Light another wooden or paper match from your candle flame and use this to light a charcoal disk. The disk will begin to spark within seconds. If the charcoal is old or damp, you may need to use metal tongs to hold it over the flame for several minutes or light the top of it in the center of the bowl-shaped depression. Most of you will realize that once the disk is lit, you don't touch it with your hands, but for beginners who have never used one before we like to add this word of caution – It is hot, just like a charcoal on a BBQ grill.
- Once the charcoal sitting in your Firebowl is lit, pull Sun Yellow energy from your candle into yourself and blow it out onto the disk.
- Add wood shavings onto the charcoal, then the pine resin and finally the sage.
- Wait for it to produce a good column of smoke and add more sage or resin if needed.
- A voice of command should be used when saying the charge verse:

"Fire and Air where you are cast,
Let no spell nor adverse purpose last,
Not in accord with me!
Cleanse this tool and cleanse its space,
Far from here send baneful trace!
Thus my will, so it be!"

Chalice: Your magickal Chalice should be a goblet shaped cup with a stem and preferably made of either glass or ceramic. Pick a Chalice that is either a Water Blue color or clear and that is either smooth or has a pattern if the pattern is not too deep. Keying your Chalice clears out any impure energy, personalizes it to you and aligns the molecules for the energy to flow in a particular direction. There are more permanent ways to key the Chalice, but for our purposes here this is how to do a quick key:

- Cup your hands on either side of the bowl part of the chalice.
- Locate a Water Blue color source.
- Begin circling Water Blue from your output hand through the Chalice, into your input hand, up your input arm, across your shoulders, down your output arm and out your output hand again.
- Circulate the color Water Blue for approximately 3 minutes, then pull your water energy back in.

To charge the Chalice you will need:

- Spring water.
- Sea Salt.
- Water Blue color source.

Charging Your Chalice to program it for keying the Plate

- Pour spring water into the Chalice until it is halfway full and add a pinch of sea salt to it.
- Swirl the mixture in the Chalice in a clockwise direction.
- Take in Water Blue energy from your color source and blow water blue energy into the Chalice while swirling the water and salt mixture clockwise.
- Then say this verse out loud blowing Water Blue energy into the Chalice and swirling the water clockwise after each line:

"Water and Earth where you are cast,
Let no spell nor adverse purpose last,
Not in accord with me.
Cleanse this tool and cleanse its space,
Far from here send baneful trace.
Thus my will, so it be."

Keying Your Plate

Keying clears any impure energy from your Plate, aligns all the molecules so the energy flows in a particular direction and personalizes the Plate to you so that other people cannot easily use it.

1. Gather your charged Firebowl, charged Chalice, and a pure cotton cloth.

2. Feel the energy of your Plate before you begin by moving your palm back and forth above it.

3. Sit in the South facing North and with your charged Firebowl and Chalice.

4. Hold your Plate upside down (dished side down) in the column of smoke from your Firebowl. Allow the smoke to drift onto the Plate for 15-30 seconds. If the Plate has been previously used by other people or for another purpose, it may take more time for the smoke to clear out the energies.

5. Pull the Plate away from the smoke and see if the smoke sticks to it (little streamers of smoke will billow off the Plate if the smoke is sticking). If not, put the Plate back over the Firebowl until the smoke sticks.

6. Smoke the bottom of your Plate in the same way until the smoke sticks.

7. Dip one corner of your cotton cloth into the water of your Chalice. Use the wet area of the cloth to wipe the top of the plate (the concave side). Start at the center of the Plate and begin wiping clockwise, moving your cloth outward in a spiral. Wipe with pressure and intention until the top of the Plate has been wiped.

8. Without stopping or lifting the cotton cloth from the plate wipe the rim of the Plate, then turn the Plate over and continue wiping the back of the Plate in the

same direction. Do not change directions once you reach the back – the wiping should be in one smooth continuous stroke.

9. When you turn the Plate over you will be wiping in a counter-clockwise direction. You may want to have another person watch you to ensure that you do not change directions. If you change directions when you start wiping the back, your Plate may actually split in half during intense magickal operations. You could end up with two very thin but completely round Plates.

10. Using a dry corner of your cotton cloth repeat the wiping procedure remembering to wipe with steady pressure and intention.

11. Test the energy of your Plate again and notice any differences.

Recipe Directions

With the Sun Candle

1. Write your list of magical directions to the Universe on a piece of paper (as described in the last recipe).

2. Place the paper on your keyed Plate.

3. Charge a Sun candle by lighting a bright yellow candle with no orange overtones, cupping your hands over the flame and saying out loud in a voice of command:

   "Child of wonder,
   Child of flame,
   Nourish my Spirit
   and Bring my aim!"

4. Place the Sun Candle on top of the paper on your keyed plate (observing fire safety precautions).

5. Sit in front of the setup for several minutes in silence, focusing your attention on the list you have written and on your goal.

6. Leave the candle burning for at least 30 minutes.

7. When you are ready to put the candle out, be sure to blow it out instead of "snuffing" it out.

8. Perform this same recipe daily to gain more magickal energy and force.

With a Magnet

1. Write your list of magickal directions to the Universe on a piece of paper (as described in the last recipe).

2. Place the paper on your keyed Plate.

3. Place a large magnet on top of the paper on the keyed Plate.

4. Sit in front of the setup for several minutes in silence, focusing your attention on the list you have written and on your goal.

5. Leave the Plate, list, and magnet setup in a secure location where it will not be disturbed until the manifestation is delivered.

6. You can return on a daily basis to do Step 4 to create more magickal energy and force.

How to Use the Results of Your Recipe

Either version of the Come Along helps create an energy matrix using your list to get the Universe started on delivering your desire. Your job now is to put yourself in the mode to receive as the level of your being attracts the level of your life. If you need to go back to previous recipes to clear out any roadblocks or issues you have that can block the delivery of your manifestation then do so. The more energy you put into this recipe, the more powerful your energy matrix will be.

Pay Some Energy Forward to Be Returned Tenfold: Pick a Price to Pay

"They deem me mad because I will not sell my days for gold; and I deem them mad because they think my days have a price."
~Khalil Gibran

Time Required: Sixty Minutes

It is quite common for people to believe that in order to receive gifts and benefits from the Universe, there is a price to pay. After all in our society, nothing is really free days. The truth however is that the Universe does not demand a price from us because it does not follow the societal rules that we do on planet Earth. Things that we consider to be miracles that are normal everyday occurrences to our manifestations coming to fruition. Instead of trying to break through and overcome this belief, it is often simpler to just go around it. One way to do this is to simple choose your own price as in this recipe.

Ingredients

- Some thinking time.
- Paper, journal or Book of Shadows and pen.

Recipe Directions

1. Spend some time considering a price that you can afford. The price doesn't have to involve money and usually works better if it doesn't.

2. In considering the price you will pay, look at the types of stumbling blocks or negative situations that appear in your life. This can help direct you towards what negative energies you might "pay out" or "give up" in your life.

3. Consider these aspects in choosing your price:
   - If you want to involve money for it to make sense to you as a price then you might donate to a charity.
   - If you don't have a hang up about money being involved, make some type of sacrifice instead. Sacrifice something you don't really need such as cleaning out a cluttered room to create sacred space in your life. You could donate unwanted items from the clutter to a charity to take it one more step. – Sacrifice doesn't have to involve physical items. It could be negative thoughts or emotional states like anger, doubt or fear. To sacrifice a thought or emotion, simply become aware of when it pops up and replace it with something else consciously.
   - Your price could be one in which you and another person both benefit as in being of service to someone else. You could do volunteer work or if you fight with your spouse a lot, pay the price of paying him or her a sincere compliment daily or offering true appreciation.

4. Make sure the price is high enough that you have to put some effort into it, yet is not so high that you avoid it, face a high risk of failure, or divert too much energy away from your manifestation goal.

5. Write down the price you choose and are committing to on a piece of paper to bring it to a physical level and make it more real.

How to Use the Results of Your Recipe

Store the paper in a sacred place such as your Book of Shadows, personal journal, or on your altar. Take your paper out daily or when you need help staying focused while waiting for your manifestation to be delivered, read it and recommit to paying your price.

[this page intentionally left blank]

Money Magick Dessert Recipes

Desserts: Meditate for Money

Practice Certainty: Walking Meditation

Practice Certainty: Mantra Meditation

"All money is a matter of belief."
~ Adam Smith

[this page intentionally left blank]

Practice Certainty: Walking Meditation

""A rich man is nothing but a poor man with money."
~W.C. Fields

Time Required: Sixty Minutes

The Principle of Certainty is a magickal principle that says that the more certain you are about a particular outcome, the faster that outcome will manifest. In communicating with the Universe and bringing your manifestation to fruition you can use this principle to remove the doubt factor. The more you connect with the Universe and Universal beings, the more secure you will be in your knowledge that they are here to help you and can help you manifest what you want. This recipe will help you develop a deeper connection and relationship with the Universe and the higher in yourself which will increase your trust and certainty that spiritual helpers are on your side. Many people have a hard time sitting through a non-moving meditation adds movement into the equation, gives you a change to tell the Universe what's on your mind, and the opportunity to get some feedback.

Ingredients

- A place to walk each day at least the length of 2 city blocks (preferably outside).
- The time to not feel rushed on your walk.

Recipe Directions

1. Decide for how long or for how far you will walk each day.

2. On the first part of the walk you will do the talking. You can talk to your guides, your totems, your angels or the Universe in general. Talk about what's on your mind, what's going on in your life, or what you want or need. Talk about anything that's important to you or that you need help with.

3. When you reach the halfway point in your walk, it is time for you to listen. Take in everything your guides or the Universe are trying to express to you. Feel your feelings, feel the sensations in your body, hear the sounds around you, smell the smells, and take in the sights. Be aware of any thoughts or feelings that come to you. Allow the magick to flow to you by becoming an instrument of listening and absorbing.

How to Use the Results of Your Recipe

If you take this walk at about the same time every day, you will establish a consistent connection with the higher. This brings magick into your life on a daily basis giving it a new richness, depth, and understanding.

Practice Certainty: Mantra Meditation

"Meditation allows us to directly participate in our lives instead of living life as an afterthought."
~Stephen Levine

Time Required: Thirty Minutes

Here is a recipe for another type of meditation you can try that is a simple and effective way to connect with the Universe and create peace, joy, harmony and manifestation in your life.

Ingredients

- At least 15 minutes of uninterrupted time.
- A comfortable place to sit free of distractions.
- A focus object such as candle, incense, fountain (optional).
- A mantra you can verbalize.

Recipe Directions

1. Find a quiet place to sit comfortably where you will not be disturbed for at least 15 minutes. You can sit in a chair or on the floor or whatever position is the most comfortable for you.

2. If you have trouble maintaining focus, you can try having a lit candle, burning incense or a fountain in front of or near you.

3. As you sit, close your eyes and feel the breath moving in and out of your body. Don't try to force your breath or breathe on purpose, just, feel your body breathing by itself.

4. At some point, thoughts will probably pop into your mind. When this happens simply let them pass through. Here is a metaphor that will help:
   - Imagine that you are sitting on the shore of a river watching boats go by. The boats are the thoughts that come into your mind. Every now and then, you will get so fascinated with a particular boat that you will want to jump on board and investigate. This is what happens when your thoughts carry you away from your quiet place on the shore. When you notice that you have been carried away by one of your thoughts, just return to your quiet place on the shore and notice your breath again.

5. Using a mantra can also help you focus and keep your thoughts from interrupting the flow of your meditation. You can chant your mantra silently or in an audible but quiet voice. An example of a mantra you could use is "Nam-myoho-renge-kyo," which means, "I devote myself to the Lotus Sutra of the Wonderful Law." You could also use something

simpler like OM.

How to Use the Results of Your Recipe

Make sure you set aside time to do your meditation every day and make it for an amount of time that you will be sure to not skip it. It is better to do a shorter meditation daily than to do longer ones sporadically. When you have finished, avoid judging your meditation by how peaceful or how disruptive it was. The important thing here is the effort you put into trying to reach a place of inner quiet. It is not as important whether or not you reached that place. Over time you will find a peace and inner quiet that goes with you throughout the day in your everyday life. The key here is that you are paying into developing your inner life and the more you do that, the more your outer life will flourish and grow.

[this page intentionally left blank]

More Magickal Resources

Kindle or Paperback on Amazon:

1. ***Witchcraft Spell Book Series:***
    - Learn How to Do Witchcraft Rituals and Spells with Your Bare Hands (Witchcraft Spell Books, Book 1)
    - Learn How to Do Witchcraft Rituals and Spells with Household Ingredients (Witchcraft Spell Books, Book 2)
    - Learn How to Do Witchcraft Rituals and Spells with Magical Tools (Witchcraft Spell Books, Book 3)
    - Witchcraft Spell Book: The Complete Guide of Witchcraft Rituals & Spells for Beginners (compilation of Books 1, 2 & 3)
2. ***Kitchen Table Magick Series***

Ebooks and Online Courses at *www.shamanschool.com*

- Wand: Air Tool
- Athame: Fire Tool
- Chalice: Water Tool
- Plate: Earth Tool
- Magical Tool: Firebowl
- Psychic Development
- Energy Healing For Self and Others

- How to Do Voodoo
- Daily Rituals to Attract What You Want in Life

Find a complete list of magickal resources on https://amzn.to/3swxvPo. These resources are constantly updated so check back often!

Free Gift Offer

To thank you for purchasing this book, I'd like to give you a

100% FREE GIFT

Learn more about your free magickal gift.

Access Your Free Gift at www.shamanschool.com

Find a complete list of magickal resources on https://amzn.to/3swxvPo. These resources are constantly updated so check back often!

About G. Alan Joel

Magick means many things to different people. The form of magick taught by G. Alan Joel for more than 30 years is steeped in tribal traditions from around the world, from both modern tribal cultures and those from the past, which have been mostly passed on through oral dialog.

At the very heart of the magick that Mr. Joel teaches is the use of Universal Laws for the benefit of self, others, and even the planet. These magickal traditions can take on many forms, including simple rituals for daily use, specific spells for particular life situations, the use of simulacra (often better known as voodoo), weather working, water witching, the use of the elemental tools (Firebowl, Wand, Athame, Chalice, and Plate), magickal self-defense rituals, and more. Also included are the use of the Tarot for divination and spellwork, divination rituals of all kinds, Spirit-to-Spirit communication, exercises for psychic development, and abundant healing techniques.

Through his 30 plus years of studying, teaching, and honing his magickal practice, G. Alan Joel has helped thousands of people successfully integrate the magickal, and seemingly miraculous, into their daily lives. In fact, one of the greatest gifts Mr. Joel has offered through his teachings is the ability for his students to always find a magickal solution for life situations that often seem impossible to solve. With magick, anything is possible in the mundane world. All that is required of the practitioner is an open mind, the desire to learn, and a willingness to pay some time and effort into his or her magickal practice. One of Mr. Joel's favorite quotes is:

"What you pay into your practice pays you back!"

While many magickal traditions have fiercely guarded their secrets from the public, Mr. Joel feels that "Magick is the birthright of every planetary citizen." As such he strives to offer magickal teachings that are easily learned and inexpensive (no excessive fees to join exclusive magickal groups or ascend up the levels of learning). He also offers techniques that are usable and effective for all who are sincere in their desire to practice magick. In essence, Mr. Joel's methods teach a form of "Every Man's (and Woman's) Magick." All are welcome, his teachings are simple yet effective, and he also offers online classes in which he helps students troubleshoot their magickal issues in an interactive setting.

Find out more about Mr. Joel's teachings here and on his website (***www.shamanschool.com***) where magickal offerings are updated on a regular basis.

Mr. Joel augments this magickal knowledge and teaching with 30 years of practice as Doctor of Chinese Medicine, including a deep understanding of herbology and acupuncture. His understanding of the healing arts deepens the magickal knowledge he teaches, as magickal healing is a major aspect of his teachings. Mr. Joel believes that while there is clearly a time and place for Western Medicine, magickal and Eastern healing techniques can be harmoniously blended in to offer people many choices for healing all types of health conditions.

About the Esoteric School of Shamanism and Magic

The Esoteric School of Shamanism and Magic was started from a desire for all people from all over the globe to be able to attend a real, if virtual, school dedicated to magick and shamanism. The aim of the Esoteric School of Shamanism and Magic is to help people create permanent, positive change in their lives through the study of esoteric magickal and shamanic knowledge. It doesn't matter what your esoteric background is, whether you started out with witchcraft, religious studies, spirituality, or candle magick, we welcome you. We believe that the Truth is the same, no matter which form you practice. We delight in all manner of shamanic schools and traditions, magickal techniques and esoteric ritual. You can visit us at ***www.shamanschool.com***, our blog at ***http://shamanmagic.blogspot.com***, or on social media via links on our website.

[this page intentionally left blank]

[this page intentionally left blank]

[this page intentionally left blank]

[this page intentionally left blank]

www.ingramcontent.com/pod-product-compliance
Lightning Source LLC
Chambersburg PA
CBHW071500130726
47997CB00006B/2409

* 9 7 9 8 9 8 5 6 2 5 7 7 6 *